EXOSKELETAL

EXOSKELETAL

poems
C.M. CLARK

SOL TION HOLE PRESS

SOLUTION HOLE PRESS

Copyright © 2019 by C. M. Clark
All rights reserved. This book or any portion thereof may not be reproduced or used in any manner whatsoever without the express written permission of the publisher except for the use of brief quotations in a book review or scholarly journal.

This book is a work of fiction. Names, characters, places and incidents either are products of the author's imagination, or are used fictitiously. Any resemblance to actual events or locales or persons, living or dead, is entirely coincidental.

First Printing: 2019
ISBN: 978-0-9967031-5-4
Solution Hole Press LLC.
www.solutionholepress.com

Book and Cover Design: Rowena Luna, LeftRight Design, Inc.
Cover Photo: C.M. Clark, "Gloria" (1982)
Author Photo Art: L.E. Clark

Also by C.M. Clark:

The Blue Hour
Three Stars Press, 2007

Pillow Talk, with painter Georges LeBar
Porky Pie Press, 2007

Charles Deering Forecasts the Weather & Other Poems
Solution Hole Press, 2012

Dragonfly
Solution Hole Press, 2016

The Five Snouts
Finishing Line Press, 2017

Acknowledgments

The author wishes to thank the editors of the following publications where selected poems appeared initially, sometimes in slightly different form.

Dogwood: A Journal of Poetry and Prose: "Dust. Sand. Earth. Silence" and "Afternoon"

The Five Snouts (chapbook, Finishing Line Press): poems in Section II

Lindenwood Review: "Starting in Xi'an"

Metonym Literary Journal: "The Stuttering Emissaries of Turfan"

Ovenbird, Issue 6: "Alice Lin's Family Reunion"

The Paddock Review: "You Will Not Make Relics"

South Florida Poetry Journal: "The Undertaking of Alice Lin" and "The Undertaker"

Travellin' Mama (Demeter Press Anthology): "Twilight"

For Anne & Laura . . .
. . . bone of my bone

Contents

I.	1
Exoskeletal	3
Lost Among the Mammals	4
The Muse of Mai	5
The Undertaking of Alice Lin	6
Haunted	7
To Market To Market	8
The Poaching	9
Under Erasure	10
The Young World	11
The Undertaker	12
Thirst	13
Congruence	14
Silk & Wool	15
Triangulate Two	16
Alice Lin's Family Reunion	17
Castor & Pollux	18
Feral	19
I Answered You in Binary	20
Sun Ji Dirgeful	21
Sleepwalking	22
Sabbatical	23
The Mountains of Hispaniola Meet the Desert of Kunlun	24
The Warden	25
What Do You See When You Look Up?	26
The Tragic End of LeeLee Mai	27
Telltale Bone	28
Song of the Coast People	29

River-Merchant's Wife Redux	30
Of The Teeth	31
In the Second Best Bedroom	32
First Word	33
Pushing East	34
The Mongols Did It	35
Mother Lode	36
The One Wife	37
Self-Portrait by Proxy	38
Division of Labor	39
The Spaces We Crawl Into	40
The Old World	41
Desire	42
Meeting Tirza	43
Konzu	44
Finders Keepers	46
Abacus	47
Manuscript	48
You Will Not Make Relics	49
Going Viral	51
Sea Anchor	52
Orphans as Teachers	53
An Apartment in Xi'an	54
The Hunt	55
Happy Trails	56
Song of the Dry Well	57
Going Vegan	58
Barbarosa	59
The Meditations of Lin	60
Song	61

II. 63

Requiem for a Headscarf 64

The Sleep Songs 66

Tirza & the Black Sisters 68

Dust. Sand. Earth. Silence. 69

Hope is a Thing with Guidelines 70

Starting in Xi'an 72

The Stuttering Emissaries of Turfan 73

Promised Wife 74

Lines in the Sand 75

Ten Years 76

Romance of the Maps 77

Afternoon 78

Dusk 79

Weather Report 80

Twilight 81

Evening 82

Early Dark 83

Insomnia 84

Commodity 85

Before Dawn 86

Mai to the Headwaters 87

Midday 88

Absence of Earth 89

Inheritance 90

Saffron City 91

Traffic Signal 92

Daylight Savings 93

I.

"... And, swooping,
you relinquish all that you have made your own,
the kingdom of your self sailing..."

— Frank O'Hara
from *"Sleeping on the Wing"*

Exoskeletal

Some creatures wear their bones
on the outside. A faltering spine,
pygmy knees, arches

fallen before flood tide and all meat-loving animals
patrolling the perimeter
of a trackless garden. When the time comes

and spiraling algorithms
emerge external, all the fainthearted
and all their postures all

slow. Funny that word. *Exoskeletal.* You think
vertebrates without lipstick, driven back
to their pre-ordained watering holes, their

acres exhausted, nothing any longer
concealed. You come to know the road begrudges its silk cargo,
its worsted loomwear or even the brutal

thinness of sloughed skin. It
is no surprise when the brittle way there comes
to prove sweeter than any calculated endgame,

any play at privacy, any
clumsy attempt to hide one's
pockmarked glory.

Lost Among the Mammals

Camels.

Yaks.

Horses.
>The dogs left before the
horses ride. One four-legged
flew in an early approach, the sheets
and stables dark, hay and bedding
turned down.

Sheep.

Goats.

The Muse of Mai

If I lived in the woods near
earth or ground, land
conducive to pine, and maybe

oak, I would spend each day counting
needles on the slash
branches, pinpoints on cones

that fell without guilt
and the sky color
brandishing the blue ever

green light.

The Undertaking of Alice Lin

My father says remember the ace of spades. He
called for the burial on a windy morning, the wind
like March gruff along the steppes, the wind

before rain and end of drought and frost and stasis. Utter
lethargy that crimps the eyebrow hairs to curl.
The crimp and cramp of organ and tissue

unused to adapt any longer. The blood
readings showed no catastrophe, but pain
oh pain said otherwise. The spade

was handled often and well, nicks in the wood,
dents in the metal curvature, hungry
for dirt for more for

earth. The tradition of this tribe, these nomads who
knew little of earth, just sand, called
for the upside first signaling

reluctance. No, no one
no one wants to heap earth on the plain
pine wood, but

we must we must turn
turn and shift the shovel
rightside, deep hungry and concave

side up. And this earth is the flip
side of reluctance – this
we must. And flowers

flowers to soften the absolute
purity of earth, the frail color and
softness saying

we must.

Haunted

This is what it means to be haunted.

Brenda Lin's mother ran to doctors or medicine
men. Or women, with bracelets and done hair, anyone to ease the brain

screw driving. Her father

never would breathe the antiseptic air. Until she
finds the note in a slaughtered book; it's the hand

writing of her mother, straight from the abattoir. This

is what it means
to be

hunted.

To Market To Market

Not lucky with food at five, Tian Mei dropped the eggs.
What kind of sorry bag was she given to hold
the dozen raw, silent in potential
over easy or sunny side up, or

the glue in meat loaf, the baste
of marbled cake. Instead a horror of viscous white
accusing yoke
accusing Mother's set mouth, mouthing

that it was alright,
but
it
wasn't.

The Poaching

Sun Ji scouted the terrain, not
likely a hostile tribe hidden behind the dunes,
the wayward random grasses. The lizard brain stirred,

pulled a face, the bully snarl all
defeating, hurling remorse in fistfuls. Soiled,
the crevices took seasons to unclench,

the spite, uncompromising. Clutching
the easy trespass – of no moment
or matter. The nettles pricked

bare calves. Summer came soon, and
at first light, one toothy dog stretched her wide mouth
hoping for chum. A devotee of stink,

that's how animals know
each other.
They recognize

to remember.

Under Erasure

Alice Lin buried her hands, burned her fingers.
Ten censors cued to do or undo
this deleting. Wood, carpet, tile, porcelain

could always be cleaned again,
and now there was time
to do it. The mosaic floor

could use re-arranging. Need now for a new
complex settling of small stones
and fabrics to be kinder underfoot.

Then the repetitions of soap and sponge,
of water and broom, the rag of a peeled eye
looking to ferret out irregularities,

the lingering stubborn pores. Stretch marks
that held the comfort of what she knew
the sentence annulled. Where now

to find consolation? Even soothing
or small talking the willful grains of erasure held back
could not re-assemble what once made

stubborn sense.

The Young World

This pencil has an odd point, Mai thought.
Made more ragged by its flawed edge, like
the tired blade that sharpened
tools when lead was young.

It seemed thin somehow, fragile.
Susceptible to be words to be lines on
paper. But,
oddly, the characters formed, formed themselves.

In another life, I owed Hesan my gratitude
and he owed me thrashed grain.
Let's remember all this
more clearly. Now

that we can.

The Undertaker

I put things in earth, ground
level and worm-deep I put
the loved arms and faces that knew

me where water will run where
the summer thunder will drench
the lank hair where dry earth

becomes dust becomes
slick becomes rising sea and level and
beneath her steps. I put

things I love to air in flame,
cauterize the silken whisker the whispered purr. I put
those things I held and nursed

those things I put to white blue heat
I put them from wick to callow to light to air
to gone. It was mine to do.

Mine

Thirst

In the imagined silence, the water girl brought
cylinders of night, not the sky's blank, not
something left to rinse the gristle the

rough tubers. Below instead the eggshell
the sharp twig nest incubated
with stilled wings, porous feathers.

Congruence

"We triangulate." Alice sees
them in her mind. The pink
one and the citrine. Tang then

sweet. The curved dunes
of Kinzu Pass seem insurmountable in this
light. But the air is light lighter

than sand.

And there's their beaten highway.
The weigh station where trucks get put on
pause and protein cells conspire

to the thirty-ninth maternal
generation. "I hear her breathe."
Alice breathes, the light curls off

her dun cheek. We are
here, the sisters commensurate,
the female gone to ground and

utterly isosceles.

Silk & Wool

1.
The umbrella that reappears as a bouquet of jonquils – or maybe daffodils – but definitely something floral, something that began as a bulb began underground. Sported like wood in a commuter's railcar, or on the dust route where weekday travelers earned their miles.

2.
Set of collectible prints, lighthouses, each a gift for five successive feasts of winter, for an acquaintance posing as her parent, where no foghorns swell, nor ocean waves, or fish, except for the fossils remaining from the eye of crustaceans. Where the only salt residue trails cheeks of aging women, the only salt matted and precipitate beneath tired feet.

Triangulate Two

Lisa Su heard little and nothing
seemed to open
her ears' inner whorls, not

so much the years the waxed the twists
or residues of the uninvited, airs
of songs brief like afterglow. And decades

after it must be Li Sam's voice so softened,
weaving the daily bits of jocular scent,
the jowls moving, the story

lost in undertow
and their maiden child grizzled with chin hairs
of her own, exhorting Sam

to speak up. She a
diaphanous device of
ear drum memory,

her tongue wrapped
around the syllables
hard enough so cold the consonants

surrender.

Alice Lin's Family Reunion

They swing in tandem, in winter
the metal ashes ache. One mother, one other

pushes, pushes,
push. *Baby*

steps, baby steps, four paws
tread. Switchback stairs to kitty-corner bed. One

white bird among birds among
birds rewriting white, circumferencing

the currents. Not uncertain
the homing birds. Collar bone coils over steering wheel.

She hunts
by scent the slant back, the left-handed turns, the one blighted tree

serrating the continent's shelf. Adrift. Reluctant
Alice Lin's teacup feet gone now

as west as feet can go before running
out of breath out of

vertical ground beneath. A swallow
of Oolong, leaf left on tongue tip,

lanterns lure blind moths with rice-paper light,
confidential breath on cheek before dinner. Paper kiss

the twin cousins, womb zones intact. The high-
waisted low one, the myopic, the macular. How

their hair greyed before the brisk fruit ripened, how
one born first, alpha dog marries dog who kicks recalcitrant stone,

buries her birthright's barely chewed
bone.

Castor & Pollux

She wasn't the favorite grandchild and never to be
the twin girl cousins who looked less alike
than bruised cherries in a bowl. Teeth

taking turns like cornrows
beneath the purse
of lips. And enjoyed more.

Feral

Sun Ji was the quintessential animal
lover. She followed the feral
dogs the cats that frequented the loading docks

the shelters. All those distorted
features, noses paler than pretty and
eyes closer,

how could they end up the sweet blood the
potter's field? Like the human
animals, the living no

longer viable, so what
if that one is her

father?

I Answered You in Binary

I answered you in binary, on off one zero. Why,
why not? There's always a train in the dream
(in the desert) in
the holy book always a sideshow of bearded ladies
of somewhere, elevated.

The stinkvines above streetlevel twin at will at first,
strangulate
to fingerbone arthritic twigs.
Approaching
a train a station's billboard

boardgame. The numb
mosaics handsign as in no name known,
deep web meme, then
like birth
sudden push of raw air like September was

always salted with cinder
ash, a hot iron's
urge,
apologies
apologize.

The ginger always helped. Even blank ground
insinuates a west pull. Hiatal hernia up and wet
wafting the nipple. Could
come down to centimeters, or

hectares. Her feet followed
each other, sand to glass
to binary blind genius. Just
on or

off.

Sun Ji Dirgeful

Sun Ji dirgeful and   voiced female
in English, bound westbound only. There's not
where you're known, not even the need
to know. Busy boy, busy bag, busy tricks beneath flaps
slid zippered in handworked compartments. Finger

mapped and tracked but lost in transit, virtual
platform, the brutal separation
this rough morning. The train,
the commuters, three-deep, the train
just pulling in out without

unnecessary lingering, retinal cues like
passengers layered like anatomically correct
cedillas, distracted by devices and failing
to notice the discarded cruelties.
Your receipts

expired coupons
cell phone photos of a newborn –
the surprise
of birth
and flash.

Sleepwalking

In the dream, a
dream, Alice Lin led
the lead, smiled and told

the student with her, *In
the dream I have been on
this path before, when*

*I walked this way I
was myself the student
in Aleppo. Familiar and less*

familiar. On the way there the
rain the hail started. We
stopped from shelter

to shelter inside when
she veered off and Alice
saw the great grey hall the white coat

the old the young
the mentor the untried
sage the jejune novitiate the cool

hall the dream in the
dream. She dreamed the
dream and I, I,

I dreamed her.

Sabbatical

1.
Somehow the pressing forward begins
when salvaged drifts obscure what would present otherwise
as sky – the footfalls unreadable with incentive removed.

Language obscures in a similar way, and Hsin-ya – neophyte
postulate to star-crossed tongues -- could barely afford a parsed adverb,
a blowsy noun. Details of

vegetation and bird life barely translucent, barely
recalling the perk of loon or sentient swallows
fly by night.

2.
She learned to kiss the closed book before reshelving – Heraclitus
taught that after the coda on change and rivers and the devil
who convinces everyone he doesn't

exist.

The Mountains of Hispaniola Meet the Desert of Kunlun

Li Po would have liked this final slice of late summer. So
where are you you you, you marauders
of close quarters? Soggy with spirit your
prisoners sweat, seeing feral dogs in the clouds, gods

in the rain brutes that run disgruntled
off the coast. They run to court the likeliest land spits,
to build resentment of all things west
African.

The village burns their rotted lot, their sharp luck.
Stealth and drive have bruised enough
for months enough. Enough. Enough
the smoke, the dirty northwest quadrant. Enough

the desert particulars that tease early,
savor the sour jerk of a million
panicked chokeholds, a million stiff necks
craning endlessly over the shoulder

in anticipation. In and out
of the low center they ride. Li Po would have liked
this new world, the wet, the dew.
Why

will no one
rid me
of these
meddlesome

beasts?

The Warden

Hsin-ya had a grandmother small
and tight. Ripe eyes and
tight lips – sorrow bow, tight apron –

ripe white where potato skins swallow
prim back, a claw-like
fist for peeling. She keeps

the keys the keys keep
her
pre-occupied, metallic with fret, seed

shells left jangling
in the claw-stretched key-dangling
pocket.

What Do You See When You Look Up?

Last carve of moon in the morning – hook
to hang last hope that dark
leeching will forestall – a line drawn

somewhere in sand, maybe near Kashgar.
Alina used Windex to wipe the eyescreen –
It might be a blue day when the dust sinks grouching.

The breathing scalp hanging her
under the sun for a different land
scape. This is moon world and

desert dark and the hooking hope
that dark virus will hang a left
somewhere before the palms

somewhere before the water.

The Tragic End of LeeLee Mai

Finding her body
of work in that weevil-waste trunk, we paused
for breath

in Samarkand. Full
need to replenish wine jugs, stock salt,
the oil's first press

and the first voice.
Aleatory, the clutter
of human.

Telltale Bone

You are the rubbed part of her right hip
joint, bone on bone when weighed on pavement, when snow drifts
on summer twilights waiting

for the bus to circumnavigate a remote neighborhood. Standing
contrapasso, the asymmetry of mordant Maidens Porch -- their
muscles never tire, grow

flaccid, their bones never press insistent, the gristle
protesting, Maremma marbled eyes gone wild in the search
for any other focus. It's only

the right hip, after all. Other parts
quiet and obedient, valiant
in their forbearance. So

when the right hip speaks, she
is made
to listen.

Song of the Coast People

So who wants to pearl dive
the dark swamp? Pull
feathers from oysters and

cod from water hissing
heat? Dive, dive and sink
like the flying fish, the suicides

that danced canals upland
in Xangtu province – years
before Soo Yang made his will

his life's mission to leave
leave his children
something

besides debt.
We remember him
as he was. Flush,

leaving large tips in
cafes that offered
a lunch

a la carte.

River-Merchant's Wife Redux

I used to think the round-eye lied. After all, male
he lied projecting the estrogen-laced plaint of that Asian girl, only
sixteen, hair grown and up, up and grown now, her

husband as far as Cho-fu-sa, and another lie, I'd sniff. Maybe
only Dunhuang, really. So the double butterflies
that hurt really hurt. Yet

in mid-October – not old August – twins
in yellow turned double helixes around
the lightpoles, an unmappable

route, hidden from all eyes except
the discreet cartographer. And at his side, Ezra
the shadow botanist, insect-master,

lay soothsayer of torque and jazz.

Of the Teeth

Of the teeth he had left, they glistened. How
in an old mouth, the recalcitrant gums, could
such saliva emerge? The brightness

of spit, and neglect, and an ill-fitting partial –
the one-way trip to Las Vegas or Samarkand or
nowhere.

In the Second Best Bedroom

It would take less than an hour. Had
to be done before
Samarkand. Before the last
toll-free exit for vehicles with multiple
axles. First, the hand

of solitaire,
dealing the stilled garments. Soiled and worn, or
worn some, some unworn, sifting the textile hand,
shifting. Alice Lin hoped
to choose well and wise. The fabrics

released their spent days. An old kitchen, or
where the camel roads rent
the air, the scent
of violet gum, clove, or
the hand-held

peripheries of lead glass. Never finding never found
the last deft touch, touched once only, traces
at a collar's corner. Fast, fastened
and finally inert. Where sleight of hand meets
landfill bound.

First Word

Beatrice Lin's first word was light, and lifelike, like
her father who saw the light of sky morning, like
the strung light in winter trees, across

rooftops and swollen winter door jambs.
Minerva Lin circumnavigated the quarter acre, the first
words tumbling like gardenia petals, *flower*

she said, and *bird* too, taking flight. Now
no parents among those on the ground, Alice
won't know – can't –

who remembers her first word. If
only someone being born today
will remember her last.

Pushing East

Alice Lin learned from the Bactrian novelists
there was a time to
stop.

The odd day moon at dawn
and full, suspicious and
full of light in draped windows.

Dim night muslin, early cats
just moving, furtive hand on door knobs
and window latches. Not

yet. Set
first before
stirring.

Alice Lin running from the typhoon
that hunted the South China Sea and
her mother's desiccation and decay

and the Yellow River flyover. A turbo
prop jet exiting the sky
for Panama City or

anywhere where all billboards
showed aborted fetuses
in vague stages of evolution.

Frog.
Amphibian. Learning to leave
the sea and grow land legs. But.

There is no leaving.

The Mongols Did It

The Mongols did it.

It was the horde that hunted the Persians.

The same horde murdered the Mandarins
and their silks unraveled
and their nails broke
heavy with opium
and tense gnawing.

Genghis sat at home in the yurt with
Borte raising
children and
tending the
five snouts, your

undeniable totems.

Mother Lode

Temujin followed the stream without
water. The changing faces, each his own, he wondered
whether his own thin beard

could be found beneath the skin. Layers
of previous anguishes, satisfying meals in years
when meat weighted the tables, the

memory of bathing in deep pools the lifted sand
residue, and his own high cheek bones and brow's contour.
It wasn't by chance his unborn fist

grasped a clot of placental blood, as if
to contain the mother link
for one orphan's moment

longer.

The One Wife

Let the record read clear.
Borte had no children, no
output of her cells, her rheumy tides. But her
sister. Yes. That was one she'd risk and stake. Hers

the arm's glissade she'd press
and sort. Aligning skinward, to delete an itinerant egg's
iron bite. Just succor for the translucent sparrow
lost to wind. Borte

the wingmaster. She choreographed.
She channeled. Borte
the last great consolation. Her wound
black braids bound

like ribbons around
a sister's miasma-wound.
Like gauze, a poultice
to lift and bind.

Self-Portrait by Proxy

Of course Borte would be so
reluctant to write, when
everything was about collapse

and the dying, the bare skulls,
the zippered throats, the
plucky orphans

that hobbled along with cheer
and appetite then
gone

in a blink of a black and
white feather, a tuft
of down.

No wonder.

Division of Labor

Temujin loved the old technology, who
said he'd never write? He
was just someone

who loved stone and sharp edges.

Borte wrote the thank-you notes.
Always the job for thin
fingers, with fine pink

nails.

The Spaces We Crawl Into

1. Between two landings of circular stairs where there's no land for miles.

2. Beneath a metal desk and the wheeling rollers of a frayed chair.

3. Behind a brocade arras where accidental murder occurred, technically manslaughter or womanslaughter.

4. Before the late mornings when the hairs seem greyer than usual, the eyes more creased more stenciled with fine crevices.

5. Besides a concrete river where water will only flow in high tide or rainy season in a desert country where rain never comes.

6. Beware the spaces we crawl into.

7. As often as we hide, we disgorge fully visible or worse yet, we blur edges with lines that define and deride our most futile silk linings.

The Old World

In Kamal's house
        the man grew old.
Older. Yet seemingly
        shriveled by the oncoming moment. Last time

Indira saw him, he had
        no spouse, no pension, no
luminous clouds bordering the rooftops.
        Do we ever have time

left?

She waited for the distance to shrink, the
dust signaling the camels' step, or
the tour bus tire's slur, killing time again

and again, nearing arrival.

Desire

Sola Abu's mother sought men
with large faces. Worshipped their broad
beard-run cheeks, high square hair magnetic

at night when loose on a pillow. She saw
the wide stance of brow bone, a pouter's
mouth. And not too old for a full plate's reward.

Mother Abu lost the younger years so
swaddled. She met them silkened young,
drew pennants in air tracking the paths far

east. Farther east and east
farther. Indelible cellular memory brought down
so to Sola. Scarf

of wool or cattle blanket abandoned
off east, her blue eyes took to looking, took
their cells their insatiable selves

with her.

Meeting Tirza

Hijab to hide
the strands that lure that
keen the want to clean
the grimed. Hijab

to hide the scalp the fuzz
the barren burned follicles fallen
radiated and severed, the
live wires of zest and flow. To

impossibly knot the printed scarf, the jewel-toned paisleys or
spring woods and patterned free creatures, woven
in hues that grow her eyes
impossibly

large.

Konzu

It was countryless and skinned of
surface DNA markers in
the Konzu corridor where we

the city the water the creatures
trespass. Maybe
the next step will land us

level with the way in the way

out.

Abu Bein is countryless
and stuck. The skin surface
map erased by sand and

shave. Who would know these pollens
or the orange melons undressed? The primogeniture
of bees is the message tonight. They alone

follow their grim slave's

trail.

Burglarized honey homing for a secret queen
and her innocent eggs. How to count four
generations of stockpiling and bites' infection,

cocoons, a final aboriginal. He's heard that
vintage tastes never question a new take made
plain. Sesame oil and ginger

would like to lunch with the

fast-breakers.

Mornings, the women hide their
deliriums. He hears they are satisfied
with vinyl eyescreens

and a brief flirtation among polyester's raucous

devotees.

Finders Keepers

There was food here – meats and the crust
of bread that has lasted and fosters the lived life.
That craves carbohydrates.

Mei remembers
the large crowd that stalked
these rooms, stiletto heels

and summer dresses.

Abacus

1. If three anonymous traders travel east with coins in their heels, will the silk measure up? Where and how far from Kashgar will they meet their match?

2. If ladies from Xi'an plan to summer in winter, where do their veils gather dust? How long will their hems trail before the water evaporates?

3. When your smart phone loses charge before the next cell tower and the outlets are three-pronged, where will you sketch your profile if the sands shift faster than your lead can scratch? Is telling the truth always the best answer to the question, "Not"?

Manuscript

Alice Lin read
the wall hanging: Silk
threads succumb
to silk road. Two cranes

and two peonies —
the buds of generation, fruit
of my womb, she thought.
Rolled and banded, aboard

the saddle storks, held
tight against the coming
sands. Would they absorb
light or leech light, fade

far beyond Kyzyl Kum, the faded
red sands before Samarkand and the
highway men. Before
colors of a different palette interrupt

the
years
of
plenty.

Milk.
And meat.

You Will Not Make Relics

This time Le-Ah brought flowers. She wrapped
them in oiled paper to discourage
the black flies, the army ants, the

rampaging legions of the under core – set
to work their spell. This chained plot she named
her garden, not hers really

just plowed and pruned by one blunt-cut grandmother
dressed in cotton and knit socks, one
never-mirrored face

to face. Yet the gardening gloves
fit hand to glove like a
glove. Le-Ah

never saw the irony in the empty day. There were clouds
obscuring the sun and their eyes gazed sideways –
the wind.

Now the day is daylight's end.
There are no geese to separate,
their plucking subdued – the light

closed in cloud cover – the shade
clear across the yard of sandgrain and
slide. Le-Ah slips

away, dogged to stealth
in the corners of traffic – last feed
last peat ember – bed and food

a reluctant camouflage.

The condo in Xi'an was spacious, the garden cool and
two flights down. In summer
insects flew, finding the pinholes

in the kitchen screen. But room to wander
from room
to room.

Movement to a space framing absolution,
cheek by jowl enumerated – and slip-streaming site
by site, small, one key cut the illusion

of security. The papers of note keep
company decomposing watermarks,
fingerprints under black light

the milestones and threshold markers,
the mule's retort. Joint tenants
of an old world

limned by paper.

The sand has a voice, the raptors,
the wings of falcons sheering cloud wool.
The spring coats of young camels, the males.

In Xi'an the desk drawers opened
and closed, the fires banked, the windows oiled
hinges oiled, newsprint, cleaning casements

with vinegar, its presence loud, loud
the street traffic, the feet of females prosaic and secular,
the males bouncing angels' virtual choirs.

Dinner tables and low-riding clouds
in spring. Basso profundo, the fathers and brothers,
the sons by marriage, like clouds interred.

The grounding horizon, the limit line –
a scarab that entered the wrong
ear, the wrong untraveled

voyagers, the singing higher, the loss
of range
and hormone and sheer

accompaniment.

Going Viral

She wished Soo Yi would
take her cancer
body elsewhere. Just stop

she thought. Stop sneaking
surreptitious jabs at your holy
apparent breast. Is that where they found

it?

Is it contagious? They
know nothing – do they? –
much, just to slice

and stab and fire
gamma rays into the heart,
the tent circle

the enemy. Does the enemy
speak our language? Does
she send spies to listen

in?

Take it with you when
the workday is done. Wipe
down your desk chair's elliptical arms,

your ergonomic keyboard. Throw
those glass slippers into the fire,
the cup you drank from. Maybe

it

is still there still and
lives even as you
won't.

Sea Anchor

Mei-Mei never knew the sea; the salt would come
in large cakes on Thursdays with ice in her town
or in summer. There, there

were only rivers, sometimes
the hint of salt seasoned
the current.

Orphans as Teachers

As the orphan elder
the last one to remember
the day of her birth –
she inherits the right,
privilege and responsibility
to sing her birthday
in praise of being born. To sing out
loud the names we
were known by,
then, by them, with no voice
left except in our
inner ears.

An Apartment in Xi'an

Last days, last day in his apartment – what fixtures were retained on the retinal wall, soon to deconstruct to

dust. Last brief notes, the old gotten-for-cheap transistor, locked tuned in to a station, songs only the gone remember

gone.

But there she was safe – knew her last slow heart exhale of someone else being the mother. Storm miles

to the south. The whine was maybe wind maybe the small cat clutched in the pull-out bed. He was so young

still.

The Hunt

The beginnings of fur the
fur trade. Pelts stacked on
pelts on animal backs a fur

sandwich an animal center
piece held joined by hide
bound bookends. The meat the milk

in the middle. The prize
in the center the blunt and tactile
cushion cushioning the meat

the meat's heart quiet yet
still, still
beating.

Happy Trails

She was pleased when the cloud cover
came. Only April but the heat returns
to Turfan and its crowded porches. She

did nothing. The absence
of absence is all there would be. A silver
vehicle in the curved driveway

or not. He is there
or he left. When did he trade
the red one in?

Song of the Dry Well

Already slipping. But
will try to remain diligent.

Quiet case of a weekend morning.
No miles today. The dogs
can rest their wagging tails the dogs
that follow. We sniff their fur, they
sniff ours, even though
it's vestigial, barely there
with light windy drift

across the ever-vigilant
wrist.

Going Vegan

Tian Mei ate lamb twice
this week – Little Lamb, who made thee so dark
and salty? Pot filling its white
enamel, a small ding on the flat handle side, sing

a song about a lamb. The second some
concoction crystallized with high-field onion and unknown
spice from somewhere unnamed
on several maps, when Ming-Ming had a little lamb was

all she'd know all
she'd remember, residue
on the
tongue.

Barbarossa

Lin had never seen anything
like it. Riding
out of the western sand,
the red

haired barbarians, with their vanilla skin
their strawberry fury. A sweet
dessert in high spring maybe,
but slightly

more dangerous. Quite enough reason
to leave. Enough
reason
to live.

The Meditations of Lin

Do scars decompose
faster than other tissue? How
do the worms like
chewing gristle?

Song

The owl breath hot

and scouting across the dunes looks
for some sand dweller, yet

now in autumn, deserted
the desert, feasts as it must

on itself.

II.

"Think of the long trip home.
Should we have stayed at home and thought of here?"

—Elizabeth Bishop
from *"Questions of Travel"*

Requiem for a Headscarf
—*For Raquel*

She brings a little sister with pink socks, her
straight teeth are homemade. They
sit at a round table, separated, to

give the lie to herdsmen and their four prophet's
palms. Kind only to a coarse rump, or lazy and snapping
sand flies, deleting invisible sapphire wings. One

by one, separately. They
shift their packs from center to side, like hair
hair that is not hair, not fur, just spider's strands, willful and

separating.

Su Li the outlander cooled her jets in the oasis pool. Paper,
scissor, rock, pliant tiles and
cardboard heatshields. The girl

with the long long hair – to her bone beltbuckle –
and darker than uninhabited coastline than night sky.
Dark like charred wood chairbacks and cloisonné partitions. She

is separate from the rest,
the travelers. We cut our hair
long ago long

before we left.

Tian Mei figured she'd set her hair
on fire. Just bow
her smooth brow into the autumn

firepit, there.
That'll do it.
Fierce. Rage. All

aglow.

When they are sick – or old – women are made
to cut their hair. Thinning and straw stick dry or
greying and unmanageable or greying
and unsightly or dyed to match

an overripe eggplant. So now – now cut now – not fashion.
No. Just flat and blunt or fringed or
shaved the hair equivalent
to ombre. To liberate the skin

the vein, unmask and sequester the main
artery in the neck or
the throat's grotto with its inflatable
scar, its epithelial zipper.

They cut their hair to anticipate
the surgeon, to expedite
the anesthetist, to finesse a finer fit
for the procedural cap.

Should I let my hair down now let
it grow down
for
now?

The Sleep Songs

Ten years passed since she slipped to sleep, she
left and left you pacing the sleep miles, she
knew the stone and sand, the storied red desert, she

knew to avoid the opal dunes. She
sleeps between the corridors of seeded tomato, the other
subterranean vegetables, the roots. Did you

imagine remorse to be so particulate?

The unfurnished arguments, the milk and meats in years
of mammal extravagance, crib to table to bed to board, the animal
famine in leap years asking where to eat, what and where to live and what,

where to place the horsehide sofa, the foxfur hammock, what hook to
hang the tribal robe. Where does reconciliation take shape? Recollection
in intimacies of personal smell: faded hairline and the thin flesh of inner
arm. On what hut wall

to study the image of one other solitary suicide?

Sleeping under your roof, where night latitudes
zigzag between capillaries and route
the practiced paths of oxygen and someone's

morning toast. Just
in the next room, so no coordination
of muscle and slack skeleton – still

the ceiling holds the matched blood,
the predictions, tendencies and
thirty-nine maternal generations.

The rain left your umbrella drying,
unnecessary. I shrug it shut and sleep –
its bright pattern backdrops

bright-still dream logic, wonderment. Where
will you go? Will it rain?
Surety –

just the sure knowledge that each day we race
the sun west, breathless for our lives – imperceptible.
Yet sure. We trespass the loud, buried sand

sure to merge with the promised mirage.
Messiah
of thirsty tongues.

Tirza & The Black Sisters

Tirza and the Black Priests' School.
Tirza and the black-moled snarl confiscating a swirling effigy. Black
the Black Sisters with hands
of bone. *Inshallah*.

Tirza beds the doll beneath mean muslin.
Eyes the line of needle's pierce, the thread
that relieves the plainness. The sleeve's wormhole
she

believes hideout enough. The red
skirt rubbed holy, fingered
currant jelly-jam by thumb chased. The bright
black

forbidden hair bareheaded. Red the lips, red
the swirl, Andalusian traces
of tamarind and cumin, lost traces
of arabesque.

En route from Cordoba pack-riding the muscle of mule's
haunch, the atoms of merchant's miles eroding
doll-feet, the fake flat heels, the lost
shoes.

The sand bats that flirted with earlobes gone
to ground beneath Kunlun dun and dust.
The bright red, the exotic bird's flutter, slap-facing the yellow
desert.

Tirza cocoons the residue, the dyed remainder,
the hand's recall of fabric, the flat Sevillian feet, the red
of red
remembered.

Tirza and the Black Priests' School.
Tirza and the black-moled snarl. Black
the Black Sisters with hands
of bone. *Allahu akbar*.

Dust. Sand. Earth. Silence.

Nature is silent. But only for a time. The bark
of caged dogs and frazzled herd animals and
animals that bear burdens

bark. The sound of me me
feed me. Where is the sun, where
is the air the food? Feed

me. Where can I find the silence the solace of the
caravan? The trek through
silent desert, needle-strewn layers

of earth. The elements call
sing their circumference.
Me. Sing me. Silence the loud

sand.

Hope is a Thing with Guidelines

1.

By now Alice Lin, the hungry ghost
reconnoitering where the slipshod waves
of St. Augustine runners run where a wedding once

was. Invincible.

Invisible in the spearheads' rustle, she reads
how mitochondrial cell mates would pair
each with blind longing – layered thick like lab slides and shelved

just so, so

two or three or
more ingenious screen names or perforated
avatars could co-

exist.

She watches for the white satin foot, the moss-blurred step,
the body-on-body jubilation – the sweetheart table
flounced over by the diaphanous

bride.

She is there then too, and parabolic
in Swarovski, and now soon, it will be her
turn, her time to repurpose and

retrofit.

2.

At what point along the x axis did Alice Lin – seduced – meet
the grunts, the foreknowing red-headed
tangle of it all?

To second

guess the weather's chest-held
hand, the overdrawn cup
of seismic tea? To be the designated

Sybil

of androgynous soothsayers, tracing petroglyphs
on sheet rock, onto phonelines left
unsecured.

The moment

lost amid the chatter – hums and fits – French
braided tweets, their hashtags zig
zagging. Thumb punch

up

wind and down slope along the Konsu Corridor:
Alice Lin's carbon footprint
in the dry season.

Shut

off the browser trail and power down. Summer
is always anxious always hot. This even the ambidextrous
lizard knows, in balance on a mute asparagus fern.

Even

the left-behind mockingbird with drooping
splayed wing knows, the odd scuttle worms brandishing
their coiled exoskeletal postures must

know.

They rule the day – overseeing
what she overlooked. The humidity
is tolerable by sundown. No records set, no records

broken.

Starting in Xi'an

Their dressmaker's dust-veil is always the same old script,
the redundant mosaic. Step

through any silk window, a corner
rubbed smooth by handprints – erased brick of foundry

the choke of ash and oxidized iron. Improbably,
rainy season came too early. A side exit

known to few already crowded with gliding arms
no stranger to henna's short-lived fade. A female voice

with a country accent. Camel hip-joints unfold
and the hooves fly to gallop between night window's ledge

and the gates of Xi'an. Already bodies
out of body jog the battle yards, board

the snub-nosed ferries, waiting for one idling ignition
to catch, turn the corner. The toll route,

familiar as skin's protein smell,
unfamiliar, as well, but stirring, stirring, stirring

and heartlessly unmapped
and heartlessly non-negotiable.

The Stuttering Emissaries of Turfan

The winding sheets and turbans they stay tucked mostly. Costumed order.
And there is ample space and steep shade by the tent folds. Dry tongues
like dune locusts click. The baristas set to strong tea-brew your first
cardamom swallow. They work

the booths, the patio tables surgically, fingerprints smudge
the honeyed ant-trails, the night's sad rehearsals of absinthe and sesame
seed. Linseed oil and old shellac. Knobbed fingers they still work folding

unfolding, unmarried mute sisters clawed as ginger root, come sullen and
sore-knuckled to burr the wool-tight carpets, virginal pink and by now,
loom-ready. They work the crowd stippled after sun damage, sharp-cut the
indigo rough, the sky-

glazed tiles. Some work the roof of spring days, some sweat
the fault line root, adding heat to the gathering traffic,
the arguing tarmac, adding salt sweat to the silica sand, glaze-blasted

and hypnotized these thousands of reluctant footfalls later. By now, you
will have spoken. Desert tried. Taklimakan proud.
Taklimakan proved. The peacocks of sundown. Eerie, dust-loud

and Homeric.

Promised Wife

The way there, Borte rode. She sat high –
the failed bench, the saddle
pinch-backing.

Only later, a horse maybe steppe-bred or small yak
bucking the midday demons, the clowns
of noon, the phase

of day's miles truncated. She looked
sideways, no, not on the mountains or
Burkhan Khaldun in the clouds at her vision's

edge, but shot her small slipstream smile
at Temujin with his long braids, coffee bright
his stare and jagged with hot spikes, acidity

and the flavor of oiled hair and
lust, too, all
so serious, untraveled but for now

and fine spun, too,
the virgin thread.

Lines in the Sand

The false day knew rough work, labored
and urging along the meat,
the multitudes. *Aleppo.* Simply

an unpronounceable name still east
of the River Amu Darya. The meal mouths
complained in jagged sighs

and the meat thighs ached, the unsteady
elevation. Lin
struggled

counting his breath
s.

Ten Years

It took Alice Lin ten years after planting, after
her tribe of cats washed so many
generations, there was no genomic memory, after

all the swallow-flying distance between
the plateaus ankle-deep and east of summer and
the aggressive spice markets to find

her mother. She traveled below
our feet and finally found
the familiar earth liberally laced

with maternal air – yeast flour
and raisins and
walnuts hard

on the teeth
the tongue.

Romance of the Maps

Only those whose feet have felt the slight
rise, the crosswords where known land marks crow's
feet, last spring's washed gully becomes

the place to turn south, leave for once
this unmarked blank and begin
the lookout for oasis emerging

from asphalt from tarmac, a push
of sand, heading not heading in
to the place where trees roost

observing protocols, folding and unfolding.

If you fold the map there at the worn crease, only
the higher elevations are visible, only
the peaks of Kunlun, the foothills

of Appalachia or the Adirondacks,
where bound heels sink arrowheads,
residue

of smoked game, a biblical offering favoring
one son
over another.

Afternoon

Sin Jin's old master belabored the ecstasies of death, the
final shout, appeal to sun storms for more
hydrogen, more. The sun

lived by desert trails. Farther,
from each old man's litany of regret, too little
love, too many days of fingers dulled

by the counting house. Their choices creep forward,
each day their tally. The tired
joints and dark kitchens, eyes

dry, unable
to
shut

even the old male cat moves
slowly to his water
bowl.

Dusk

A younger sister made it her habit to sing
to her mother's bones. Twice yearly
when the summer escaped on an outgoing tide when
the full moon of seething green raised grass heads. The bones

that housed her replicating cells shifted, knew
her steps, her sandaled feet – turning once
to recollect the cadence, they met: one voice
instructing the next.

Weather Report

They tell us grandfather went back
to China. He won't be back. They tell
us, "We had some rain here."

"Here, the front just came in."

One last act of housekeeping before departing Dandan Oilik. The desert promised little
in the way of cabinetry.

Small porcelain knobs, utilitarian shoeboxes
emptied of soft slippers. Here was
one old residue of daywear, pointless now

the lost blush and peony, somewhere gone east
with the housewife of shelved moisture,
sweat stains beneath the ribcage

the small of a back. This
would shroud Mei-tai. Left
with the unborn

fetuses, the waxed lilies.

Twilight

Her obsession became full-bodied
and round – a melon straight
from the tilted garden tracing

the lowland's curve. The silt-heavy
rivers helped carry her throat's sore lump
along, careening rock to rock, riverbed

to tired tributary. Even slogging these foothills,
distant Loulan no more than nightmare
than memory, she nursed each sour swallow.

A stunted child fed on gruel, barely
grain, barely milk, barely
water and redolent with clanging insects.

Evening

Rough fingers probe the sleeping mats
and their party blossoms, a
grandmother's wide-lipped poppies, a bluebell
someone's demure nod. Three chairs, four-

legged, unknown tree anonymous stain, someone
thought the finish moneyed, even
resplendent. Were there water rings marring
the side tables? Someone's night sweats

a shadow for May flowers? Someone
could furnish a newlywed's first hut, if only
the dusty sheets would be
silent.

Early Dark

The dreaming tigers spread their feral sweat, coy atoms
homesteading the unmapped air
complete with flowerbeds

and charcoal grill. The lead walkers known, knew
the middle ground. So long
as they walked, kicked dust and

sand, neutralized pheromones and phlegm in dry throats
clearing. At night, she heard
her name, corners rounded by sleep, a potted plant

where wall met floorboard. Her name. The rest
the slang of private augurs
untranslatable.

Insomnia

Between starpoints she realized lying
bareback on the cold sand, drew
the heat from spinal tissue, from muscle's

ligature, sure sign nothing died nothing sank
toward stasis. The heat circuited through flesh points to
ground crust, silica's endpoint, her

nighttime's entropy. Lying
against cold leather against animal
skin, pressed back toward sofa bed back,

she gathered lingering twigs, somnambulist
counting cards, backward
toward fields toward mountains, how

the land mapped how
middle age played her luck
her hand.

Commodity

Outside the Kunlun Pass, An-Lee knew a man, she
said tall, like the cliché and greying, females
and click beetles, the ambush

of honey mead, sparkle
in a drowsing eyelash. Her knees
felt cold to the touch, legs below the knee

cool. Unshaven and the rub of nylon – eyes
always watched the fabric press
press along the salt, the ochre sand.

Before Dawn

What with May and the drying grasses, prelude
to what desert months will reap and belittle
what cheap coverings and harnesses made dreary

with inadequacy. In the high plains, straw ground only
mumbled the temporary and worthless, the
sniff of green somewhere absent, the sniff

the high speed ailerons bearing down a wet
washing. We poke at
the unintentional remainders. Food

for random nomads, and those who let loose
their home flocks, clowders, covens, assorted
gaggles of new geese bearing down.

The dog-eared remnants,
the dry spring.

Mai to the Headwaters

Mai and I fingered stained
glass geometries. Triangular
wedding sets of pure sunstone

fitting each to one, then
prying down rough
prongs. We liked the hand

of it. The lines of honeycomb,
the virgin blue, the citrus.

Midday

Colorblind on a mountain road. Lin
reshaped his iris diameter, looking
for a break in the fog. Green

seemed a resuscitation of lowland fields, the
terraced markings of family and
truculent neighbors. But green

nonetheless, and green's white-haired grandmother,
green's fragrant newborn, sharp with placental residue,
spring green's flirtatious sister, she

who lost a tooth, no one knows how. The blue shadows
where grass had been chewed raw by stealthy creatures and
their furtive intentions. All

cool color
fog
warmed.

Absence of Earth

They bury the dead in the mountain
on a slant facing the freelane, sightless eye
attracting the sun. The mounds

don't rise, no need when the rough old earth
urges its own elevations. No straight lines
in nature, nothing

but curves along the treeline, the crow's trajectory. How
deep do they need to dig to find
the forest crib, root's cradle?

Inheritance

Alice Lin recognized her grandmother's dress, though
the armholes gaped vacant and the tea-garden
figurines along the hem talked to

themselves, no legs long and veined
listening. The rag pack folded and
unfolded, more strictly to compress the particolored

mixed bag, patterns, prints, plaids, outsqueezed
the spring air from the coastal fields
the furrows. Here

the chest buttons
carried
their own tune.

Saffron City

Karakum ground shifts forward, says *there's more*
to my breath than sand. Those gaudy trees, that hot yellow. The sign.

The sprig. The tabebuia not
pronounced as it seems. The spring. So

amorous, such buttercup leaves, such
gauze, such wounds, such striated tissue.

They neglect to cipher the sun, the stove's
element. The origin. Yellowface

defines the sky, the spleen. The warning. Yellow
colored her skin's jaundice. So Windsor blue

they handpainted her dress. The fake.
The yellow the sign, the signpost

of Gaochang on the outskirts.
Rest the pollen-flecked eyelids, rest

the eyes that ate apricots, the apples and peaches.
The dunes a wanton's back, a fan-dancer's muscled calf.

Flesh and yellow ochre and
the tang of ox-fur's musk,

meat juice on jaw, on
iridescent whiskers.

Traffic Signal

A source of relief. And
quaint.
Hsin-ya's mother would order

the downturning world
by reading signs. She'd circle
the vacant square in Xi'an, alphabetize

the menus, configure the dialogues overheard,
the conjoined signals. Cunning how precious
argot would press for her its linear way along

the declarative sentence, its matrix
of ley lines and thunderheads over the desert. And vertical
as the Kunlun peaks, abrupt syntax, a choir's

punctuation and end stop. To be –
and the body, noon day's dreamt arcana of codes
and chemistry, dragging the traveler ever

on and forward. The body – the scared
recalcitrant dog.

Behind her and seven steps back,
the sand mites
the carnal hawk's flight overheard, like

monsters of breath, a month's saliva residue in a dry mouth,
scorched bedpillow invisible, immediate, burred
in the scalloped dunes that lie ahead

the voice only, and young
for the date in fragrant Samarkand – and swaddled
in lucky yellow sleeves, she would

catch a glimpse. Birds
summon, fingers
gesture, the cohort of rose attar, there

there, the wordless young
intone.

Daylight Savings

It was the cheat time, the fox months and weeks.
Water moccasin belching after feathers and beak. Even
the hours are compromised. From the coy sneer

that destabilizes – she likes the smirk –
to the jarring single
sign. She sings,

the belt, the rub of steel on steel singes
sting
s.

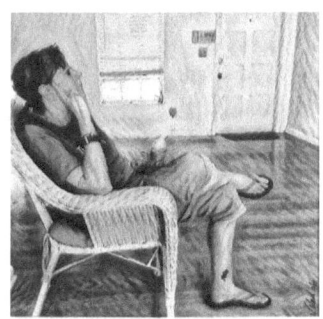

C.M. Clark's poetry has appeared in *Painted Bride Quarterly, Prime Number Magazine, The Paddock Review, Ovenbird, Metonym Literary Journal, The Lindenwood Review, Dogwood: A Journal of Poetry & Prose,* the *South Florida Poetry Journal, Spire Light* and *Gulf Stream* magazine. Her work has also been selected for Demeter Press's anthology, *Travellin' Mama,* and for the *South Florida Poetry Journal Anthology.* Clark was runner-up for the Slate Roof Press Chapbook Contest and Elyse Wolf Prize, a finalist for the Rane Arroyo Chapbook Series, and semi-finalist for Molotov Cocktail Press's Shadow Award. She also served as inaugural Poet in Residence at the Deering Estate Artists Village in Miami, and has been a featured presenter at the Miami Book Fair. Author of full-length works *Charles Deering Forecasts the Weather & Other Poems* (Solution Hole Press, 2012) and *Dragonfly* (Solution Hole Press, 2016)), Clark's recent chapbook, *The Five Snouts,* was published by Finishing Line Press (2017). Clark has a Ph.D. in English from the University of Miami, and has taught writing and literature at Miami Dade College.

www.ingramcontent.com/pod-product-compliance
Lightning Source LLC
Chambersburg PA
CBHW030452010526
44118CB00011B/896